D0001515

On the Job

Librarians
In Our Community

Michelle Ames

Discard
NHCPL

PowerKiDS press™

New York

NEW HANOVER COUNTY
PUBLIC LIBRARY
201 CHESTNUT STREET
WILMINGTON, NC 28401

For Ellen

Published in 2010 by The Rosen Publishing Group, Inc.
29 East 21st Street, New York, NY 10010

Copyright © 2010 by The Rosen Publishing Group, Inc.

All rights reserved. No part of this book may be reproduced in any form without permission in writing from the publisher, except by a reviewer.

First Edition

Editor: Nicole Pristash
Book Design: Greg Tucker
Photo Researcher: Jessica Gerweck

Photo Credits: Cover Anderson Ross/Getty Images; p. 5 Ableimages/Getty Images; p. 7 © Jim Craigmyle/Corbis; pp. 9, 24 (left) © www.iStockphoto.com/Dennis Morris; p. 11 © Gonzalo Azumendi/age fotostock; pp. 13, 24 (right) © www.iStockphoto.com/Kelly Boreson; p. 15 Andy Crawford/Getty Images; p. 17 © www.iStockphoto.com/Jani Bryson; p. 19 Shutterstock.com; pp. 21, 24 (center) Henrik Sorensen/Getty Images; p. 23 © David Pollack/Corbis.

Library of Congress Cataloging-in-Publication Data

Ames, Michelle.
  Librarians in our community / Michelle Ames. — 1st ed.
      p. cm. — (On the job)
  Includes index.
  ISBN 978-1-4042-8072-4 (lib. bdg.) — ISBN 978-1-4358-2458-4 (pbk.) —
ISBN 978-1-4358-2459-1 (6-pack)
  1. Librarians—Juvenile literature. 2. Libraries–Juvenile literature. I. Title.
  Z682.A53 2010
  020'.92—dc22

                                    2008053793

Manufactured in the United States of America

Contents

A librarian is a person who works in a **library**.

A library is a place to find and read books.

Libraries are found in almost every town and city.

Public libraries are libraries that anyone can use.

There are also libraries in schools. **Students** go to the library to do their work.

People often bring library books home. Librarians check the books out on a computer.

LENDING LIBRARY
AND
ENQUIRIES
→

A librarian reads books to groups of kids who visit the library.

This student is having a problem using a computer. A librarian will help her.

Librarians have to carry **stacks** of books.

Librarians take time to help us learn at the library.

Words to Know

library

stack

students

Index

Web Sites

Due to the changing nature of Internet links, PowerKids Press has developed an online list of Web sites related to the subject of this book. This site is updated regularly. Please use this link to access the list:

www.powerkidslinks.com/job/librarian/